RATE YOUR SKILLS AS A MANAGER

A Crisp Assessment Profile

A FIFTY-MINUTE™ SERIES BOOK

CRISP PUBLICATIONS, INC.
Menlo Park, California

RATE YOUR SKILLS AS A MANAGER
A Crisp Assessment Profile

CREDITS
Editor: **Michael Crisp**
Layout and Composition: **Interface Studio**
Cover Design: **Carol Harris**
Artwork: **Ralph Mapson**

Copyright © 1991 by Crisp Publications, Inc.
Printed in the United States of America

English language Crisp books are distributed worldwide. Our major international distributors include:

CANADA: Reid Publishing Ltd., Box 69559—109 Thomas St., Oakville, Ontario, Canada L6J 7R4. TEL: (905) 842-4428, FAX: (905) 842-9327

Raincoast Books Distribution Ltd., 112 East 3rd Avenue, Vancouver, British Columbia, Canada V5T 1C8. TEL: (604) 873-6581, FAX: (604) 874-2711

AUSTRALIA: Career Builders, P.O. Box 1051, Springwood, Brisbane, Queensland, Australia 4127. TEL: 841-1061, FAX: 841-1580

NEW ZEALAND: Career Builders, P.O. Box 571, Manurewa, Auckland, New Zealand. TEL: 266-5276, FAX: 266-4152

JAPAN: Phoenix Associates Co., Mizuho Bldg. 2-12-2, Kami Osaki, Shinagawa-Ku, Tokyo 141, Japan. TEL: 3-443-7231, FAX: 3-443-7640

Selected Crisp titles are also available in other languages. Contact International Rights Manager Suzanne Kelly at (415) 323-6100 for more information.

Library of Congress Catalog Card Number 90-85866
Rate Your Skills As A Manager
A Crisp Assessment Profile
ISBN 1-56052-101-5

This book is printed on recyclable paper with soy ink.

Now that we are into the nineties, some people are claiming that the previous decade was a period of excesses and that *downsizing*, *reorganizing*, and *lowering expectations* are due. Others, with more positive attitudes, recognize that adjustments need to be made, but view the nineties as an opportunity that must be challenged with new goals and higher expectations.

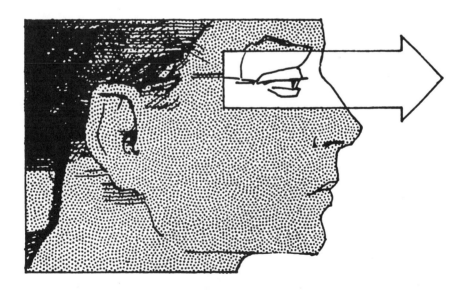

LOOK TO THE FUTURE

CONTENTS

INTRODUCTION

This is a self-help management publication, but it is more than a simple book. The material is developed around twelve recognized management competencies or techniques. As a reader you have an opportunity to rate yourself in each area by taking a self-assessment. When all are completed, you have built an intriguing personal profile of your management skills. Do not let this unique approach fool you into thinking this book is without content substance. You will learn the essence of professional management as you take inventory of your skills and your potential to develop.

You will need to read this book with pencil in hand because there are exercises and ratings to complete as you progress through the pages. After completing the text portion of the book, you will be asked to complete a management profile on yourself. Done honestly, this profile will reveal your strengths and weaknesses and give you specific suggestions on how to make improvements.

Don't rush! Take your time and enjoy the process. Once you have completed your profile you will be in a position to begin making changes that will help you be a winner, even in tough times.

Good luck!

Michael S. Crisp

SHOULD YOU BE READING THIS BOOK?

If you currently occupy a management or leadership position the answer is a resounding YES. If you are in the process of preparing for a management position, the answer is YES. If you are simply interested in learning more about management and leadership, perhaps to use in other aspects of your life, the answer is still YES.

The Crisp Management Development Profile will introduce you to twelve critical competencies that constitute the essence of good management. Of course, such a small book cannot cover all facets of management. For example, no attempt is made to cover the theoretical side of management. Neither does this book deal with financial matters though it is obvious that many management roles require a strong foundation in accounting, statistics, and the accumulation and interpretation of computer-based data.

What this book does provide is a critical review of *key* management functions, a *summary of what a manager should* know, and a *self-appraisal* on how she or he is performing at the present time.

THE MANAGEMENT PROCESS

Management practitioners and scholars vary widely in their definitions of the management process. These differences are usually nothing more than a choice of words. Some consolidate similar functions into broad categories—others prefer an extensive list of individual functions.

Management is the process of working through individuals and groups to accomplish organizational objectives. A top manager works through people. To do this effectively requires the ability to communicate, motivate, and lead. The higher one climbs up the management ladder the more important her or his immediate staff becomes. Appraising results is also a key management function.

Not all excellent managers have academic degrees. Many work their way into key roles through experience and self-learning. Indeed, a few universities who offer a rigid MBA program heavily oriented in the direction of theories, computers, and economics turn to the more practical aspects of management before degrees are awarded. Those in charge realize that their graduates will start near the bottom where practical knowledge and application count most.

The twelve categories (techniques) presented in this publication, are at the heart of the management process no matter how it may be defined. Once learned and practiced, they spell success and advancement.

PART

I

The Twelve Management Challenges

Challenge 1

Are You A Creative Planner?

PLANNING IS GOAL-SETTING

Many people envision front-line employees showing up for work with little required job preparation. Managers, on the other hand, are normally viewed as people who have been reviewing and revising plans about what needs to be accomplished. Successful managers are always planning. It is a conceptual process that goes with being a manager.

Planning is thinking that precedes doing. It is concerned with establishing organizational goals and objectives and with preparing specific plans and schedules to see them accomplished. From the list below, select the three statements you view as most important, and rank them.

☐ 1. Interpreting goals and objectives passed down from above as the result of planning performed at a higher level.

☐ 2. Gathering the thoughts and ideas of the employees who are directly involved, as well as your own thoughts and ideas.

☐ 3. Formulating and issuing policies and procedures to accomplish goals and objectives.

☐ 4. Examining alternatives and selecting the activities and programs that will lead to successful results.

☐ 5. Establishing timetables and completion targets in keeping with priorities.

☐ 6. Determining standards of performance and how results will be measured.

☐ 7. Identifying the resources necessary for task accomplishment—people, time, money, material—and determining their availability.

Although managers must concentrate their planning on the over-all performance of their operation, they must also initiate, define, plan, implement, and evaluate individual projects (within the larger framework) in order to reach their goals. To be an excellent manager, you must be able to successfully direct a number of critical "projects" simultaneously.

My top three rankings are:

1. Number _____

2. Number _____

3. Number _____

PLANNING IS AN ATTITUDE

Managers usually know whether or not they are good planners. If the planning process gets them involved in how they can accomplish the goals of their organization, chances are excellent those managers will devise a successful plan based upon critical priorities. If, however, a manager finds it difficult to become involved or has trouble viewing his or her plan conceptually, it will be more difficult to do an outstanding job.

Superior planning means understanding conceptually what is required to successfully complete a project insofar as quality, time, and cost are concerned. Please check the planning steps listed below that you are confident you could accomplish in your area of responsibility.

Planning Steps

☐ Establish the project objective.

☐ Choose a basic strategy for achieving the objective.

☐ Break the project down into subunits or steps.

☐ Determine the performance standards for each subunit.

☐ Determine how much time is required to complete each subunit.

☐ Determine the proper sequence for completing the subunits and aggregate this information into a schedule for the total project.

☐ Design the cost of each subunit and aggregate costs into the project budget.

☐ Design the necessary staff organization, including the number and kind of positions, and the duties and responsibilities of each.

☐ Determine what training, if any, is required for project team members.

☐ Develop the necessary policies and procedures.

---

*For details on *Project Management: From Idea to Implementation*—a book by Marion E. Haynes—see the information in the back of the book.

CASE # 1: DECISION

Victor is an excellent restaurant manager, especially when it comes to relationships with employees and customers. Yesterday, in a three-hour session, Victor's zone manager (Jane Tracy) announced that his restaurant was scheduled for a light remodeling starting the first of next month. All of the improvements would be made without closing down the operation. Complaints from customers should be anticipated. Victor would receive a blueprint presenting the details in a few days. An outside project manager would be assigned to handle all aspects of construction. Victor's responsibility would be to maintain the best possible overall operation during the projected four week period. The key, according to Jane, will be the way Victor handles his employees.

Victor does not consider himself to be highly skillful in conducting group meetings. Because of this, he has decided to schedule required individual appraisal meetings with each of his employees ahead of time and use this occasion to announce and discuss the remodeling challenge. To Victor, this is creative planning because it will kill two birds with one stone.

What do you think of Victor's plan? Please write out your answer and compare with that of the author on page 102.

_____

_____

_____

WHEN THE BUSINESS ENVIRONMENT BECOMES MORE COMPETITIVE THE BEST WAY TO GIVE YOUR FIRM AN EDGE IS THROUGH MORE CREATIVE PLANNING.

MANAGER'S SELF-INVENTORY SCALE

It is now time to critically rate your planning skills on a specific scale that will be used in all twelve categories. As you do this, ask yourself these questions.

- How do you stack up as a planner with managers in positions similar to yours?

- Do you sometimes receive compliments from others on your planning skills?

- Is setting short- and long-term goals and then organizing a plan to reach them something you enjoy?

Please follow these instructions carefully.

On a scale of from 1 to 10 rate your level of performance during the past year in the area of planning. Do this by circling the appropriate number on the scale below.

- If you circle 1, 2, or 3 you are saying you need substantial improvement to reach your potential as an excellent planner.

- If you circle 4, 5, or 6 you are telling yourself you need considerable improvement in developing your planning skills.

- Should you circle 8, 9, or 10 you are indicating that you need only a little or no improvement. By all criteria, you are an excellent planner.

If you are not currently occupying a management position, rate yourself on how well you plan aspects of your current job.

MANAGER'S SELF-INVENTORY SCALE
Planning

Low									High
1	2	3	4	5	6	7	8	9	10

Challenge 2

How Skillful Are You At Delegating?

THE DO-IT-YOURSELF MANAGER
WHO HATES TO GIVE UP CONTROL

HOW WORK GETS DONE IN ORGANIZATION

Management is a leadership effort to integrate and effectively use a variety of resources to accomplish an objective. It applies to all organizations, whether they are businesses, hospitals, or political entities. Managers will do well to remember there is no one best way to plan, organize, or control. Each manager must continually increase his or her knowledge of management concepts and draw upon them until a winning combination is found that fits him or her, the people supervised, and the work involved.

One factor is central, however, to every management task. That factor is DELEGATION. The manager must know what is expected of his or her unit, when it is expected, and how to best employ his or her human resources to obtain the desired results. This means assigning work in a planned and thoughtful way.

> Delegation is giving people things to do. Management is accomplishing organizational goals by working through individuals and groups. It is easy to see that the two are closely entwined. And it is obvious that the manager who is not delegating is not managing.

Delegation, of all the skills and activities of a manager, is one of the most indispensable.

REVIEWING YOUR SKILLS

Here is an opportunity to learn how well you delegate. This scale will help identify your strengths and determine where improvement would be beneficial. Circle the number that best describes you. The higher the number, the more the statement describes you. When you have finished, total the numbers circled in the space provided.

1. Each of my employees knows what I expect of her or him.

   7 6 5 4 3 2 1

2. I involve employees in goal-setting, problem-solving, and productivity improvement activities.

   7 6 5 4 3 2 1

3. I place my personal emphasis on planning, organizing, motivating, and controlling, rather than doing tasks others could do.

   7 6 5 4 3 2 1

4. When assigning work, I select the assignee thoughtfully.   7 6 5 4 3 2 1

5. When a problem occurs on a project I have delegated, I give the employee a reasonable chance to work it out for him/herself.

   7 6 5 4 3 2 1

6. When I delegate work to employees, I brief them fully on the details with which I am familiar.

   7 6 5 4 3 2 1

7. I see delegation as one way to help employees develop their skills, and I assign work accordingly.

   7 6 5 4 3 2 1

8. I support and help employees in emergencies, but I do not permit them to leave work for me to do.

   7 6 5 4 3 2 1

9. When I assign work, I stress the results desired, not how to accomplish them.

   7 6 5 4 3 2 1

10. When I delegate a project, I make sure everyone concerned knows who is in charge.

    7 6 5 4 3 2 1

11. When delegating work, I balance authority with need and experience.

    7 6 5 4 3 2 1

12. I hold my employees responsible for results.   7 6 5 4 3 2 1

TOTAL _____

A score between 72 and 84 suggests you are on target. A score between 48 and 71 indicates you are getting by, but could improve. Anything below 48 means you need to make changes.

CASE # 2: OVERSTATEMENT

Phyllis and Jeff are discussing comments made by an outside consultant who is conducting an in-house seminar on management skills. The comment made by the consultant was: "Delegating is by far the most underrated skill possessed by managers. More managers fail because of their inability to delegate than any other, including communication."

Phyllis said: "I really disagree with this guy, Jeff. My experience has demonstrated to me that communication and financial abilities far outweigh the ability to delegate. I think he made an overstatement he would have trouble defending."

Jeff replied: "I would go along with him, Phyllis, for one reason. Unless you know how to effectively delegate the work and responsibility to others, you would never have time to plan and truly manage. Put another way, you are only free to manage after you have delegated as many tasks and responsibilities as possible. I give delegating top priority among all management skills."

Do you defend Phyllis or Jeff? Why? Write out your answer and compare with that of the author on page 102.

_____

_____

_____

> WHEN MARKET CONDITIONS FORCE AN ORGANIZATION TO TIGHTEN UP ITS OPERATION, MOST EMPLOYEES ARE WILLING TO ACCEPT MORE RESPONSIBILITIES.

MANAGER'S SELF-INVENTORY SCALE

Listed below are excuses most managers give for not delegating. Please check those you would apply to yourself.

☐ I can do the work in my unit better than anyone else.

☐ I don't know the techniques of delegating.

☐ My employees won't like me if I expect too much of them.

☐ I am not certain to whom I should delegate.

☐ It is easier and quicker to do things myself.

☐ We can't afford to make any mistakes.

☐ Management expects me to handle important things myself.

☐ My employees can't be trusted.

☐ We are seriously understaffed.

☐ Most of our decisions are made under crisis conditions.

Based upon your response to the last three pages, please rate yourself as a delegator.

MANAGER'S SELF-INVENTORY SCALE
Delegating

Low									High
1	2	3	4	5	6	7	8	9	10

How Well Do You Do In Maintaining Control?

KEEPING PRODUCTIVITY HIGH

Many highly promotable employees turn down supervisory or management positions because they feel inadequate when it comes to controlling people, finances, and resources. These excellent producers do not want the responsibility of supervising those who may have difficulty conforming to acceptable standards, keeping track of financial matters, and protecting the resources of the organization. In other words, they prefer to produce rather than assume the responsibility of control.

On the other hand, other people enjoy setting performance standards and helping people reach them. They eliminate control problems by making sure employees understand what is expected, teaching them how to achieve expectations, and providing constructive feedback. These managers enjoy "being at the helm." They thrive on the recognition that can come from finding and correcting leaks in an operation. They love to report "savings" to superiors based upon the effectiveness of their controls.

> IN TOUGH TIMES, EMPLOYEES NEED MORE SECURITY, NOT LESS. A GOOD WAY TO PROVIDE THIS SECURITY IS TO LET THEM KNOW YOU AND YOUR COMPANY ARE UNDER CONTROL. IN SHORT, THEY ARE WORKING FOR A WINNER.

TIGHT SHIP EXERCISE

In most organizations, running a "tight ship" is considered a goal that managers should understand and support. This is because properly executed, it results in higher employee productivity, better use of material resources, and excellent control over budgets. It is doubly important to be able to run a "tight ship" during tough periods when showing acceptable results might be difficult to achieve.

The following exercise is designed to start the process of deciding just how prepared you are to run a tight ship.

	Yes	No
1. Can you keep control over your operations without stifling employee self-motivation?	☐	☐
2. Can you quickly spot and correct unacceptable behavior in a subordinate without becoming personally upset?	☐	☐
3. Do you consider it a compliment when someone says you run a tight ship?	☐	☐
4. Can you spot a problem in its infancy and make a correction before it grows into a major concern?	☐	☐
5. Can you keep discipline among your employees without becoming heavy-handed?	☐	☐
6. Can you prove that there is less employee inefficiency in your department than there is in similar sections?	☐	☐
7. Have you set up the right kind of financial reporting (systems) so you can spot trends quickly in order to make corrections easier?	☐	☐
8. Do you enjoy spending time analyzing reports to spot variances and opportunities for improvement?	☐	☐
9. Can you approach a problem-employee in such a way that she or he is willing to make behaviorial change while respecting you for helping?	☐	☐
10. Can you run a tight ship without being so "picky" that employees consider you as an interloper instead of a good manager?	☐	☐

TOTAL YES ☐ **NO** ☐

Seven or more "yes" answers is a signal you may have your operation under proper control.

CASE # 3: PREFERENCE

Herb is considered a laid-back branch manager with a "tough touch." That is, most of the time everything flows along with little supervision, but occasionally, Herb pulls up on his discipline line so tight that for a day or so, the entire branch shakes a little. Employees who have been around for awhile seem to get used to his tough style but newer employees often react in negative ways and their productivity drops for a few days.

Kathleen is known as a person who is always on top of things in her branch. A new employee soon discovers that she knows everything that is going on and too much relaxation or socialization is soon corrected through "soft" counseling. Yet, there are times, usually on Friday afternoons, when Kathleen seems to change her style and everyone relaxes and has fun. Everyone knows, however, that on Monday, Kathleen will be on top of things again.

Which of the contrasting management styles do you defend? Is it better to be like Herb with a consistent permissive style and an infrequent tightening up? Or do you prefer Kathleen's style of a consistent discipline line with occasional relaxation?

_____

_____

_____

You are invited to compare your thoughts with those of the author on page 102.

MANAGER'S SELF-INVENTORY SCALE

Do Employees Take Advantage Of You?

Every operation has its own perimeters of control. Some organizations, like a nuclear energy generating plant, have extremely rigid controls. An advertising agency, in contrast, is highly participative and requires less stringent rules. As you rate yourself, keep in mind the working environment you manage and ask yourself these questions:

- Have you fostered a sense of involvement and ownership on the part of your employees?

- Are you consistent in maintaining your discipline line?

- Are you able to create a team spirit in which employees take responsibility for controlling themselves?

Please rate yourself on your ability to establish and maintain a productive but controlled working environment.

MANAGER'S SELF-INVENTORY SCALE
Control

Low									High
1	2	3	4	5	6	7	8	9	10

Challenge 4

How Goal-Oriented Are You?

GOALS! GOALS! GOALS!

Most successful managers are highly goal-oriented. They react in a positive way to the organizational mission. They set goals with their employees and have their own personal objectives. Goal-setting and goal-reaching is an integral part of their management style.

Goal-oriented people have four common characteristics:

1. They recognize that self-motivation comes from establishing reachable goals. These successful people do not wait around for others to motivate them. If others do not provide motivating goals, they provide their own.

2. They have learned that there is a satisfying fulfillment when a meaningful goal is reached. They believe in setting daily goals because they feel better at the end of the day. They have weekly goals because reaching them establishes that progress has occurred. And although they may not talk about them, these individuals usually have long-term or life goals that give them a sense of mission.

3. Goal-oriented people have little patience for those who do not set goals or respond to goals created by superiors. Because of this, these managers recognize the value of the "team" approach to productivity—they understand that forming a team instead of a "work group" pulls all employees together to reach a common goal.

4. They recognize the importance of involving the people who must achieve goals after their formation.

ORGANIZATIONAL GOALS

All organizations have established goals. That is why slogans such as "Quality is Job One" (Ford), and "We Try Harder" (Avis) are important. The only problem is that such slogans do not always become converted into a sense of mission and are not always fully articulated to all employees.

Although some organizations claim their goals come from their departmental MBO (Management By Objectives) programs, where departments submit individual plans that eventually become corporate goals, more admit that goal-setting at the departmental level has a greater impact upon employee motivation and productivity. That is why successful management has started to give their departments more and more autonomy to form "teams" or "independent units."

Departments or teams increasingly learn to set their own goals through meetings where everyone is a full partner. During these meetings they participate in setting time limits on completion, determining the rewards for success, and suggesting how their efforts can fit into the long range strategy of their organizations. In other words, through the dynamics of the group process they undertake assignments and tasks to make their team a winner. In doing this, they provide their own motivation to establish and reach quality standards, even if it means competing aggressively with other "units" that may be performing identical tasks.

PERSONAL GOALS

Successful managers/leaders are not only skillful in setting "team goals" with employees, they are true believers because they set goals for themselves. Their goals usually fall into three classifications:

1. **Career goals—** those that will create a career path that conforms to their own desires, values, and comfort zones.

2. **Lifestyle goals—** those that will eventually give them the kind of leisure and/or family life they seek.

3. **Life goals—** those that combine "dream wishes" for both their working and retirement years.

By reading this book "with a pencil," you are in the process of building a *MANAGEMENT DEVELOPMENT PROFILE* for yourself. This will happen on page 92. After you complete it, chances are you will discover one or more weak categories in your management tool box. For example, you may discover you need to improve your skills in delegating, negotiating, or problem solving. If so, making improvements in such categories will constitute goals. In other words, your profile will provide you with some new goals that can enhance your career future.

CASE STUDY

CASE # 4: ATTITUDE

John is recognized as an outstanding manager. Two years ago, after receiving various awards for his achievements, he set a goal of becoming a zone manager where he would supervise other managers in the role he currently occupies. Soon after setting this goal his firm started retrenching. About a month ago it became obvious that his goal would be impossible to reach within the time expectations he had set for himself.

After dealing with the frustration of not achieving his goal, John also lost his motivation. Talking to a co-worker, he said: "Trish, I've decided not to set career goals in the future. The way the economy is going, it seems like an exercise in futility. Why should I frustrate myself? Life is too short to build expectations and have them smashed. For the next few years I'm just going to float—hang on to this job and coast along until things start picking up."

What is your reaction to John's attitude? If you were Trish, how would you reply? Write out your ideas and compare them to those of the author on page 102.

_____

_____

_____

_____

_____

_____

_____

_____

MANAGER'S SELF-INVENTORY SCALE

Judging Yourself

Before rating yourself on your ability to manage personal goal setting, ask yourself these questions:

- Would I like to learn more about how to set and manage goals?

- Is having a goal my best way to stay motivated?

- Am I sufficiently flexible to revise my goals when, due to circumstances beyond my control, they become unreachable?

- Am I a competitive person?

- Do I know how to involve my employees in goal setting?

- Do I agree that setting goals is almost the only way to achieve self-motivation?

- Am I satisfied with my career, lifestyle, and life goals?

Some people are so goal-oriented that they run the risk of becoming workaholics. Others, are so lacking in motivation that they find work a drag. If you feel you are making the most of your goal setting abilities without overdoing it, do not hesitate to give yourself a high rating. When it comes to self-motivation, only you have the answer.

MANAGER'S SELF-INVENTORY SCALE
Goal Setting

Low									High
1	2	3	4	5	6	7	8	9	10

Challenge 5

How Do You Rate Your Counseling And Coaching Techniques?

VALUABLE MANAGEMENT TOOLS

A manager who wishes to influence, direct, teach, and motivate employees needs to develop expertise in two essential skills: counseling *and* coaching. Anytime an employee comes to you with a personal problem that is having a negative impact on his or her productivity, *counseling* is in order. Whenever a manager needs to teach an employee a new skill, restore motivation, or help the individual establish goals, *coaching* is the tool to use.

Counseling is a *supportive* process that assists employees to define and work through personal problems that affect job performance. Counseling usually takes place when an employee comes to his or her manager. Sometimes, however, intervention by the manager is welcome by the individual.

Coaching is a *direct process* by a manager to train and orient an employee to the realities of the workplace and to help that individual remove barriers to optimum work performance.

At times counseling and coaching overlap. Many techniques are applicable in both areas. It is, however, important to know when one approach produces better results than the other.

Please study the next two pages to insure that you have clarified the differences.

COACHING OR COUNSELING?

COUNSELING IDEAS

WORK SITUATIONS THAT MAY REQUIRE COUNSELING

Check any that you have personally encountered:

☐ 1. Reorganizations

☐ 2. Layoffs—counseling for those who are laid off *and* those who are not

☐ 3. Demotions due to organization changes

☐ 4. Salary freezes; decreases in salary, status or responsibility

☐ 5. Employee faced with other career opportunities inside or outside of the organization

☐ 6. Employee faced with no career opportunities inside the organization

THE BENEFITS OF COUNSELING

Why should you improve your counseling skills? Read each of the following statements below. Do you think they are true or false? Check your opinion and compare it with that of the author at the bottom of the page.

True **False**

☐ ☐ 1. Improves productivity of your business when employees feel listened to and supported.

☐ ☐ 2. Reduces turnover when employees feel they can vent their thoughts and feelings and deal with problems openly and constructively.

☐ ☐ 3. Makes your job easier by giving you warning of resistance or problems that may occur following changes.

☐ ☐ 4. Increases efficiency of your business when you understand the motives and needs of each employee and how he or she will react to organizational events.

☐ ☐ 5. Reduces conflict and preserves self-esteem when parties are really listened to.

☐ ☐ 6. Helps you solve problems before they occur.

ALL STATEMENTS ARE TRUE

COACHING IDEAS

WORK SITUATIONS THAT MAY REQUIRE COACHING

Check any that you have personally encountered:

☐ 1. Orientation and training of a new employee

☐ 2. Teaching a new job skill

☐ 3. Need to explain standards of the work unit

☐ 4. Need to explain cultural norms and political realities of the organization

☐ 5. Simple corrections to performance are required

☐ 6. Goals or business conditions change

THE BENEFITS OF COACHING

Why should you improve your coaching skills? See if you agree with the author by deciding which statements are true and which are false. Compare your answers with those of the author at the bottom of the page.

True **False**

☐ ☐ 1. Makes your job easier when employees build their skill levels.

☐ ☐ 2. Enables greater delegation so you can have more time to truly manage rather than ''do for.''

☐ ☐ 3. Builds your reputation as a people developer.

☐ ☐ 4. Increases productivity when employees know what the goals are and how to achieve them.

☐ ☐ 5. Develops sharing of leadership responsibilities.

☐ ☐ 6. Positive recognition and feedback increases employee motivation and initiative.

ALL STATEMENTS ARE TRUE

CASE # 5: INTERVENTION

Listed below are two situations you face as a manager in a major corporation. In which case would you use counseling? In which case coaching? Read both cases, make your decision, and then be prepared to defend your answer.

1. Jack is a highly creative and aggressive marketing manager under your supervision. You like Jack but recognize that he pushes himself and others to achieve goals. Recently, you have been receiving complaints that indicate he may be pushing too hard for the long-term good of the firm. You would like to see Jack develop his natural leadership ability in a more sensitive style, but you do not want to put a damper on his efforts.

2. Jane has an outstanding track record as a credit manager with your firm. You know of two occasions where competitive firms have set out signals they would like to have her on their team. For the last two months, however, Jane's behavior and productivity have not lived up to her previous standards. You suspect she is having family or personal problems of some kind and decide to make yourself accessible by inviting her to have lunch with you.

I would use counseling ☐ coaching ☐ in the first situation. My approach would be to:

_____

_____

_____

I would use counseling ☐ coaching ☐ in the second situation. My approach would be to:

_____

_____

_____

You can compare your answers to those of the author by turning to page 103.

MANAGER'S SELF-INVENTORY SCALE

Guiding Others

How you go about rating yourself on your counseling and coaching techniques depends upon the management position you occupy and your past experience. If you have had many opportunities to sharpen your techniques you might use the following guidelines:

- If you feel comfortable with your *style,* give yourself 2 points.

- If you have developed into an excellent listener, give yourself another 2 points.

- If you have learned to select the right location, time, and approach in doing your counseling and coaching, give yourself an additional 2 points.

- Add another 2 points if you know when to counsel and when to coach.

- If you have evidence your efforts have brought about excellent results, you might give yourself 2 more points and rate yourself as a 10 on the scale below.

- If, however, you have had little experience in counseling and coaching, and you rate yourself under a 2 in any of the 5 categories above, a lower rating is in order.

- Should you feel you have a high potential but, as yet, your opportunities have been limited, do not hesitate to give yourself a 5 rating.

MANAGER'S SELF-EVALUATION SCALE
Counseling and Coaching

Low									High
1	2	3	4	5	6	7	8	9	10

Challenge 6

What Is Your Track Record When It Comes To Hiring Successful Employees?

THE STAFFING CHALLENGE!

As a manager, you may or may not be significantly involved in the staffing process. Some managers have complete control over who is hired or transferred into their departments, others must select from those sent by the Human Resources Department. Regardless of your present situation, as you move up in the organization selecting the right people will become increasingly important.

Staffing includes much more than simply filling a vacancy with the best available individual. It also involves determining organizational long-term personnel needs; orientation and training; transfers and reassignment; rotation; performance evaluations; and, on occasion—terminations. The moment a vacancy or personnel change is in the offing, experienced managers ask themselves:

- If the function performed by the exiting employee is absolutely necessary?

- Could the tasks be divided among other employees?

- What skills are missing among the staff that a new employee could provide?

- What kind of person will contribute most to greater productivity?

- Is someone being trained to eventually take my job?

The goal of every manager should be to hire, develop, and maintain the most cohesive and productive staff possible. Sex, race, age, or physical handicaps cannot play a part in the selective process. The practice of first come, first hired should be avoided. Screening written applications and interviewing should be done studiously.

MAKE CAREFUL HIRING DECISIONS

TWO KINDS OF INTERVIEWS

Employment interviews can be divided into two different patterns. First is the guided approach, second is a less structured, or unguided approach. For the inexperienced interviewer, a guided pattern is usually best. For example, a novice might consider using the check list below. The fictitious word CASSI is a device to help the manager rate all five categories in each interview.

JOB QUALIFICATION CHECK LIST

	Yes	No
C COOPERATIVENESS (Will the applicant make an effort to work well with the staff?)	____	____
A ATTITUDE (Does the applicant have a good work attitude? Does he or she really want to produce?)	____	____
S SKILLS (Does this person have all the specific skills to match the job opening?)	____	____
S STABILITY (Is the applicant seeking a permanent or interim job?)	____	____
I INTEREST (Has the applicant expressed high interest in the job?)	____	____

Although no system is perfect, any guided pattern has the advantage of providing at least some objectivity. Of course, the interviewer must ask the right questions so that the above characteristics surface.

CASE #6

CASE # 6: CHOICE

Alex was pleased when management selected his assistant, Carla, to supervise a newly created department. It was a compliment to Alex who had encouraged and trained Carla. But losing Carla meant many new problems for Alex, so his first question was: "How can I turn Carla's vacancy into an advantage?"

Alex, a methodical manager, listed seven factors that he felt were involved in the selection of Carla's replacement. Select the three you would consider most important and compare with those of the author on page 103.

☐ **1.** Determining who would have responsibility to train and orient the person hired.

☐ **2.** Making sure the best qualified individual is chosen during the screening process.

☐ **3.** Using the vacancy as an opportunity to reorganize the department to make better use of several employees' skills.

☐ **4.** Improving the cultural mix of the department.

☐ **5.** Building better relationships with your department by hiring a positive person.

☐ **6.** Discussing the needs of the department with other employees to discover ways in which greater productivity can be achieved.

☐ **7.** Examining the possibility of reassigning existing staff members for either cross training or promotion.

MANAGER'S SELF-INVENTORY SCALE

Selecting Winners

The more staffing experience you have had the easier it should be to rate yourself in this category. For example, if you have hired a number of people in your career, and a majority have lived up to your standards, give yourself a high rating.

No matter how much experience you have had, please ask yourself these questions before circling the appropriate number on the scale.

- Do you know how to analyze job requirements?

- Can you develop an interview plan?

- Are you experienced at using questions to gather pertinent information?

- Do you know how to avoid violating equal opportunity laws?

- Can you objectively evaluate qualifications against job requirements?

- Do you know how to document the selection process?

- Do you know your personal prejudices and can you control them?

MANAGER'S SELF-INVENTORY SCALE
Staffing

Low									High
1	2	3	4	5	6	7	8	9	10

Challenge 7

How Do You Rate Yourself As A Team Builder?

TEAM PRODUCTIVITY

Excellent managers in all types of organizations often seem content with the performance of their "group" without trying to mold their employees into a "team." This often occurs because they are satisfied with current productivity and do not consider what *could* be accomplished with a "team" approach. They refuse to acknowledge that other managers doing similar tasks with the same technology somehow have better productivity because they establish a climate where people achieve their potential and consider themselves as part of a "team."

Team building is a little like baseball. The leader (manager) has the responsibility of selecting players, coordinating efforts, and providing the leadership to win the game. But to be successful:

• Players must be committed to helping the team.

• Communication, trust, and mutual support is a must.

• A reward system recognizing individual and team achievements must be established.

• A game plan must be developed, accepted, and followed.

A leader gets her or his team to first base through planning, organizing, motivating, and controlling. The team gets to second base when everyone focuses on agreed upon goals. Third base is reached with open communication. The team scores a run (or victory) when goals are achieved.

So what is the real difference between a "group" and a "team"? Please turn to the next page.

GROUPS VS TEAMS

GROUPS	TEAMS
☐ Members think they are grouped together for administrative purposes only. Individuals work independently; sometimes at cross purposes with others.	☐ Members recognize their interdependence and understand both personal and team goals are best accomplished with mutual support. Time is not wasted struggling over ''turf'' or attempting personal gain at the expense of others.
☐ Members tend to focus on themselves because they are not sufficiently involved in planning the unit's objectives. They approach their job simply as a hired hand.	☐ Members feel a sense of ownership for their jobs and unit because they are committed to goals they helped establish.
☐ Members are told what to do rather than being asked what the best approach would be. Suggestions are not encouraged.	☐ Members contribute to the organization's success by applying their unique talent and knowledge to team objectives.
☐ Members distrust the motives of colleagues because they do not understand the roles of other members. Expressions of opinion or disagreement are considered divisive or non-supportive.	☐ Members work in a climate of trust and are encouraged to openly express ideas, opinions, disagreements and feelings. Questions are welcomed.
☐ Members are so cautious about what they say that real understanding is not possible. Game playing may occur and communication traps be set to catch the unwary.	☐ Members practice open and honest communication. They make an effort to understand each other's point of view.
☐ Members may receive good training but are limited in applying it to the job by the supervisor or other group members.	☐ Members are encouraged to develop skills and apply what they learn on the job. They receive the support of the team.
☐ Members find themselves in conflict situations that they do not know how to resolve. Their supervisor may put off intervention until serious damage is done.	☐ Members recognize conflict is a normal aspect of human interaction but they view such situations as an opportunity for new ideas and creativity. They work to resolve conflict quickly and constructively.
☐ Members may or may not participate in decisions affecting the team. Conformity often appears more important than positive results.	☐ Members participate in decisions affecting the team but understand their leader must make a final ruling whenever the team cannot decide, or an emergency exists. Positive results, not conformity are the goal.

ATTITUDES OF AN EFFECTIVE TEAM BUILDER

The following attitudes support team building. This scale will help identify your strengths, and determine areas where improvement would be beneficial. Circle the number that best reflects where you fall on the scale. The higher the number, the more the characteristic describes you. When you have finished, total the numbers circled in the space provided.

1. When I select employees I choose those who can meet the job requirements and work well with others.	7 6 5 4 3 2 1
2. I give employees a sense of ownership by involving them in goal setting, problem solving and productivity improvement activities.	7 6 5 4 3 2 1
3. I try to provide team spirit by encouraging people to work together and to support one another on activities that are related.	7 6 5 4 3 2 1
4. I talk with people openly and honestly and encourage the same kind of communication in return.	7 6 5 4 3 2 1
5. I keep agreements with my people because their trust is essential to my leadership.	7 6 5 4 3 2 1
6. I help team members get to know each other so they can learn to trust, respect and appreciate individual talent and ability.	7 6 5 4 3 2 1
7. I ensure employees have the required training to do their job and know how it is to be applied.	7 6 5 4 3 2 1
8. I understand that conflict within groups is normal, but work to resolve it quickly and fairly before it can become destructive.	7 6 5 4 3 2 1
9. I believe people will perform as a team when they know what is expected and what benefits will accrue.	7 6 5 4 3 2 1
10. I am willing to replace members who cannot or will not meet reasonable standards after appropriate coaching.	7 6 5 4 3 2 1

TOTAL _____

A score between 60 and 70 indicates a positive attitude toward people and the type of attitude needed to build and maintain a strong team. A score between 40 and 59 is acceptable and with reasonable effort, team building should be possible for you. If you scored below 40, you need to carefully examine your attitude in light of current management philosophy.

CASE # 7: CRITERIA

Assume you have been assigned a special project by your superior. Your immediate job is to select the best person for promotion into a new position.

Hank comes to mind first. He is technically superior to the others in the group. He has great discipline in his department. He is excellent at delegating. In addition, he has seniority.

Sandy pops into your mind next. She is younger than Hank but has proven herself to be even better at getting productivity from employees than Hank. She does a lot of coaching and gains employee commitment. She seems to enjoy her role more than others. And she has great enthusiasm.

What criteria should you use in choosing between Hank and Sandy as a team leader? Based upon the criteria, who would you select? See what the author would select on page 103.

_____

_____

_____

_____

> ONE WAY TO INCREASE EMPLOYEE PRODUCTIVITY DURING ADJUSTMENT PERIODS IS TO ACCEPT THE CHALLENGE OF BUILDING MORE TEAM SPIRIT WITHIN DEPARTMENTS. IT IS AMAZING HOW PEOPLE RALLY TO THE CAUSE WHEN THEY SEE THE BIG PICTURE.

MANAGER'S SELF-INVENTORY SCALE

Rate Yourself as a Team Leader

It is difficult for any manager to rate himself or herself as successful team leader. Those who have been members of both sporting and/or management teams in the past may have some advantages over those who find the concept foreign to them. On the other hand, others seem to use the team approach in a natural way without having been connected with a team. Please read the following statements before you rate yourself on the scale below.

- If, as a manager, you have rejected the "team idea" in the past, consider giving yourself a rating between 1 and 3 until you give it a chance.

- If you have seriously tried the team approach with what you feel was limited success, consider giving yourself a rating between 4 and 5.

- If you are committed to the team approach and have had success in making it work for you both in the past and now, consider giving yourself a score on the high end of the scale.

- If you have yet to occupy a management position, rate yourself on your *potential* as a team leader and then subtract 3 points to compensate for lack of experience.

MANAGER'S SELF-INVENTORY SCALE
Team Building

Low									High
1	2	3	4	5	6	7	8	9	10

Challenge 8

Are You Good At Negotiating?

NEGOTIATING IS A SIGNIFICANT MANAGEMENT TOOL

Negotiation takes place when we try to satisfy our needs despite someone else controlling what we want. In most cases it can be a healthy process and both parties come out winners. Because of its delicate nature, there are other times when the process bogs down and haggling takes over.

From the list below, check the three areas where you most frequently become involved in negotiations.

☐ Price and/or delivery dates of resources.

☐ Labor or sales contracts.

☐ Seeking a raise in pay and benefits.

☐ Negotiating to keep a top employee from leaving.

☐ Establishing new policies or philosophies.

☐ Adjusting a marketing plan.

☐ Breaking a previous relationship.

☐ Personally negotiating with another firm that wants you to join them.

☐ Convincing a co-worker you are right.

☐ Getting an adjustment to your departmental budgets or revenue targets.

There is a danger that you may become involved in a problem without recognizing it as an opportunity for negotiation. When this happens you may not be as well prepared to use "win-win" negotiating techniques as would otherwise be the case.

MY REACTION TO DISAGREEMENT, CONFLICT, AND NEGOTIATION

Following are several statements about personal reactions to disagreement and conflict. Circle the number that best describes you. The higher the number, the more you agree with the statement. When you finish, total the numbers you circled and write it in the space provided.

	Strong Agreement					*Mild Agreement*				
It doesn't bother me to question a price or seek a more favorable exchange than offered.	10	9	8	7	6	5	4	3	2	1
I have nothing to lose in seeking a better deal if I do it in a reasonable way.	10	9	8	7	6	5	4	3	2	1
Conflict is a fact of life and I work hard to resolve it.	10	9	8	7	6	5	4	3	2	1
Conflict is positive because it makes me examine my ideas carefully.	10	9	8	7	6	5	4	3	2	1
In resolving conflict, I try to consider the needs of the other person.	10	9	8	7	6	5	4	3	2	1
Conflict often produces better solutions to problems.	10	9	8	7	6	5	4	3	2	1
Conflict stimulates my thinking and sharpens my judgment.	10	9	8	7	6	5	4	3	2	1
Working with conflict has taught me that compromise is not a sign of weakness.	10	9	8	7	6	5	4	3	2	1
Satisfactorily resolved, conflict often strengthens relationships.	10	9	8	7	6	5	4	3	2	1
Conflict is a way to test one's own point of view.	10	9	8	7	6	5	4	3	2	1
GRAND TOTAL _____										

If you scored 80 or above you have a realistic attitude toward conflict, understand negotiation, and seem willing to work to resolve it. If you scored between 50 and 79 you appear to be dealing fairly well with conflict, but need to work toward a more positive approach.

If your score was below 50, you need to first understand why, and then work hard to learn techniques of conflict resolution.

CASE # 8: STYLE

Marci and Malcolm have been invited by top management to apply for a management promotion that carries higher benefits and prestige. The position requires considerable negotiating with outside resources and buyers.

Marci feels she is best qualified because she sees herself as a smooth negotiator who is adept at avoiding conflict. She has no fear of the negotiating process but tries to keep it at a professional level without inviting conflict.

Malcolm also enjoys negotiating, but sees conflict as a natural part of the process. He is good because he knows how to resolve conflict. Malcolm also knows the importance of using a win/win approach. For example, Malcolm loves to challenge the position of the other party in a forceful manner and make them scramble to justify their position, but he understands the importance of developing an outcome both parties can live with.

Accepting that in all other areas Marci and Malcolm are equally qualified for the new management job, which one do you feel would serve the organization best? Why? Read the author's opinion on page 103.

_____

_____

_____

> FOR SOME MANAGERS, "TOUGH TIMES" IN THE
> MARKETPLACE CAN MEAN RENEGOTIATING
> CONTRACTS ALREADY IN PLACE. FOR OTHERS, IT
> MEANS NEGOTIATING MORE FAVORABLE CONTRACTS
> IN THE FUTURE. IN EITHER CASE, NEGOTIATING
> SKILLS BECOME MORE IMPORTANT.

MANAGER'S SELF-INVENTORY SCALE

Rating Yourself as a Negotiator

You may find it difficult to rate yourself as a negotiator—especially if you have had little opportunity in the past to practice the techniques involved. Asking yourself the following questions will assist you in circling the most appropriate number in the scale from 1 to 10.

- Have you lost out in the past because you backed away from the negotiation process?

- Is the process of negotiating distasteful to you?

- Have you frequently turned negotiating over to others?

- Have you avoided learning and practicing the techniques and strategies of negotiation?

- Would you prefer a management role where negotiating would be at a minimum, perhaps confined to dealing with employees on one side and upper management on the other?

If you gave "yes" answers to three or more of the above questions, it may be a signal that you should rate yourself 3 or under. If you gave yourself only 2 or 1 "yes" answers rate yourself higher. If you have had limited opportunity to practice the art of negotiating but you sense you would be good at it, rate yourself somewhere below the middle of the scale.

MANAGER'S SELF-INVENTORY SCALE
Planning

Low									High
1	2	3	4	5	6	7	8	9	10

Challenge 9

Are You A Superior Problem-Solver?

SIZING UP A PROBLEM

Completing the Manager's Profile in this book requires many decisions. Taken seriously, these are important decisions because they deal with your career success. Several are not, however, critical in the sense that they may cost thousands of dollars if the wrong answer is made. The decisions you are making in this book to build your profile are for self-evaluation purposes only.

Many highly qualified people refuse opportunities to become managers because they don't want to face the problem-solving responsibilities that go with a manager's job. Often these people are not aware that they can learn proven techniques that can help them to make good decisions. Others are simply fearful of taking the risks involved.

In most situations, management problems divide themselves into four classifications:

> Small people-centered problems.
> Major people-centered problems.
>
> Small job-centered problems.
> Major job-centered problems.

Small problems in both categories require careful consideration so they don't grow into big problems. Normally they can be disposed of in a short period of time without making an in-depth study.

Major problems often require a system or step-by-step procedure that takes time to gather facts, consult with colleagues, and additional considerations. Six typical steps include:

1. Recognize the problem.
2. Gather all possible data.
3. Analyze the data from all perspectives.
4. List the options.
5. Make the decision.
6. Adhere to follow-up procedures.

Do you take an organized approach to solving problems similar to the above?

YES ☐   NO ☐

PROBLEM-SOLVING CHECKLIST

Assume you are involving a team in making a major decision. If you complete the checklist ☑ below you may discover there are many more angles or facets in this type of decision-making process than you had expected.

I plan an agenda directed to finding a solution.	_____
I keep the group on track.	_____
I set and stick to ground rules for participation.	_____
I break down big problems into "bite-sized" chunks.	_____
I complete each step before moving to the next.	_____
I return to the previous step if progress bogs down.	_____
I know which technique I'm using at each point.	_____
I trust the process and keep on it as long as it works.	_____
I don't mix methods from different processes.	_____
I include all people or units affected.	_____
I openly consider divergent ideas as valuable input.	_____
I accept and integrate all views and feelings.	_____
I write down all thoughts, suggestions, and input.	_____
I keep a public running record of group discussion.	_____
I keep all material visible to all group members.	_____
I know which questions to ask at each step.	_____
I draw out complete answers from all present.	_____
I discipline myself to listen and respond.	_____
I assign distinct roles in the meeting.	_____
I stimulate the group's synergy and creativity.	_____
I seek agreement between divergent positions.	_____
I test for consensus as points are agreed upon.	_____
I summarize conclusions before closing.	_____
I assign responsibility for action as appropriate.	_____

HOW MANY BLANKS DID YOU CHECK? _____

There are many books that can help you professionalize your decision-making techniques and improve your track record. One such book is *Systematic Problem-Solving and Decision-Making* by Sandy Pokras. See page 100 for further information.

PROBLEM SOLVING IS RISK-TAKING*

Problem solving requires taking risks. Sometimes taking the risk is well worth doing. At other times it may not be. Deciding whether or not to take a risk is a decision unto itself. Here are some guiding principles to consider:

1. *Learning and personal growth require taking risks.*

A life lived to maintain security, by holding onto the status quo, eventually becomes a prison. Personal development requires loosening your grip on what you already have mastered and moving beyond your ''comfort zone'' into the unknown.

2. *Take only those risks where you can handle the loss.*

All risky situations can result in loss. In a worst-case scenario, if the loss would be catastrophic (materially or emotionally), don't take the risk *in its present form.*

To build self-confidence, start small. Don't begin by plunging into risks with heavy penalties. As you gain experience, harsh choices often become less burdensome. For example, putting your job on the line is less stressful after you've already made some successful career changes.

3. *Adjust risks that are too much of a gamble.*

Consider improving the odds and reducing the chances of loss by obtaining more information, spreading the liability, hedging your bet, and gaining more control over the outcome of your decision.

4. *Accept that the price of risking is occasional failure.*

Don't demand a perfect track record of yourself or others. One employee put $100,000 at risk in a promotional campaign. When she sheepishly told her boss about the negative outcome, the boss asked what she had learned from the experience. In surprise she asked, ''Do you mean I'm not fired?'' ''How could I even think of firing you?'' the boss said. ''I've just invested $100,000 in your education!''

Are you willing to take risks in keeping with the above?   Yes ☐   No ☐

Rate Your Skills As A Manager

---

*For additional information investigate the book *Risk Taking—A Guide For Decision Makers* by Herbert S. Kindler, Ph.D. see the back of the book.

CASE # 9: EXPANSION

Your company has earned consistent profits by marketing a small line of products throughout your city. As marketing manager, the CEO wants your recommendations on expanding to other cities. You have 30 days to investigate the facts and make a clear decision. As part of your decision, he also wants you to give your views on whether it would be best to expand with the firm's capital (somewhat limited) or go into franchising.

The problem is complicated because your immediate superior (between you and the CEO) is against expansion of any kind.

What process would you follow in making your decision?

_____

_____

_____

Compare your thoughts with those of the author on page 103.

IN DIFFICULT TIMES, MANAGERS ARE CALLED UPON TO MAKE MORE DECISIONS. THOSE WHO HAVE PREVIOUSLY IMPROVED THEIR PROBLEM-SOLVING TECHNIQUES AND ARE WILLING TO TAKE CALCULATED RISKS, FIND THEMSELVES IN THE DRIVER'S SEAT.

MANAGER'S SELF-INVENTORY SCALE

Decision-Making Time

Before you rate yourself at the bottom of the page, ask yourself these questions?

- What has been your problem-solving track record in the past? Are you doing better today?

- Do you use a problem-solving system? Is it working to your satisfaction?

- When you are forced into making a ''gut'' decision (no time to gather facts) do you do so without excessive anxiety? Are you usually right?

- Are you frequently guilty of sweeping important decisions under the carpet? Do you regret it later?

- Do you agonize over key people decisions to the point that it has a negative impact on your other management skills?

What do your responses to the questions at the bottom of pages 59, 60, and 61 suggest about your skills and where you should rate yourself on the scale?

MANAGER'S SELF-INVENTORY SCALE
Decision Making

Low									High
1	2	3	4	5	6	7	8	9	10

Challenge 10

How Professional Are You?

PROFESSIONALISM = QUALITY

To rate yourself on the *degree* of professionalism you possess as a manager requires insightfulness and a few guidelines. According to Webster's New World Dictionary, a professional is one who is worthy because she or he meets certain high standards.

- Professionals seek excellence in themselves and those who work for them. *Quality* is their goal.

- Employers place a high value on their services.

- Professionals conduct themselves in such a way that others look up to them and respect their judgment.

- They are knowledgeable. A professional manager keeps up to date and never stops learning how to be a better one. He or she seeks continuous personal growth and advancement.

- Professional managers adhere to accepted ethical standards.

Do you view management as a profession? Are you proud to be a professional manager? Consider the following pages and then rate yourself in this sensitive but vital area.

> THE TEMPTATION TO DEVIATE FROM HIGH QUALITY PRACTICES IS PRESENT DURING BOTH NORMAL AND TOUGH TIMES. THOSE WHO STICK WITH THEIR STANDARDS EVENTUALLY WIN THE RACE.

WHAT QUALITY IS AND IS NOT*

Here is a list of attributes describing what quality is and is not. Use this list to identify your personal and professional responses to the quality challenge. Add your own ideas at the bottom.

QUALITY IS:	QUALITY IS NOT:
A philosophy	A quick fix
Conformance to perfection standards	Goodness
Prevention	Merely inspection
Following specific guidelines	A ''close enough'' attitude
A lifelong process	A motivational program
Commitment	Coincidence
Supported by upper management	Randomly adopted
A positive attitude	A watchdog mentality
Agreement	Do your own thing
Willing communication	Isolated data
Understanding your processes	Guessing
Identifying opportunities for error	Detecting errors in end products
Add your own:	Add your own:
_____	_____
_____	_____
_____	_____

*Chart reprinted from *Quality At Work* by Diane Bone and Rick Griggs. Crisp Publications, Inc.

QUALITY PLUS ETHICS

Public concerns about ethical practices in business usually relate to issues like embezzlement, accepting bribes, or poisoning the atmosphere. Such examples suggest managers' problems with ethics consist of nothing more than violations of clear-cut, well-defined laws, rules, and codes of conduct.

Managers, on the other hand, mostly cite examples that arise directly from routine business practices. Their ethical concerns are about relationships and responsibilities where correct decisions are not perfectly clear, and there are no hard, fast rules to follow.

One set of relationships and responsibilities is directly related to employees, and includes such areas as discipline, performance appraisal, safety, and the administration of reward systems. Another set is concerned with customers and suppliers, and includes the intricate aspects of such elements as timing, quality, and price. Ethical dilemmas also arise when managers have conflicts in values with superiors or peers over such things as strategy, goals, policy, and administration.

Whatever the viewpoint, good ethics means good business. Successful organizations and managers take ethics seriously. They reason their way through ethical dilemmas to acceptable solutions. Some organizations and managers give the appearance of success for long periods in spite of hidden unethical practices. The news is replete, however, with stories of the fallen heros and devastated organizations that ultimately result from this deception.

"DON'T BE TEMPTED TO COMPROMISE YOUR ETHICS"

CASE # 10: BEHAVIOR

Assume you have a close friend who occupies a management role in your organization. The position is similar to yours. You work with this individual every day. In recent months you have noticed that this person:

• Increasingly turns out sub-standard work.

• Occasionally violates safety regulations.

• Fabricates excuses when absent.

• Plays politics with performance appraisals.

• Takes credit for the ideas of others.

For some time you have suspected that this individual was an alcoholic. A few days ago this was confirmed by a member of the person's family.

What is the ethical thing for you to do? Write out your answer in the spaces below and match your thoughts with those of the author on page 104.

_____

_____

_____

_____

_____

MANAGER'S SELF-IMPROVEMENT SCALE

Rating Yourself as a Professional Manager

You are now ready to rate yourself as a professional on our scale of from 1 to 10. In doing this, you may wish to follow the guidelines below:

1. Ethics is not the whole story in being a professional but it is important. If you take ethics into consideration in all of your management decisions, give yourself three points on the scale.

2. If you are constantly improving your knowledge about management—learning new techniques—attending seminars—reading self-help books—and making a daily effort to put them into practice, give yourself another 3 points. You can't be a professional if you are just treading water.

3. If you believe in setting and achieving quality standards, give yourself another 3 points.

4. If you gave yourself 3 points in each of the above categories, you might take the last step and rate yourself as a 10.

MANAGER'S SELF-DEVELOPMENT SCALE
Professionalism

Low									High
1	2	3	4	5	6	7	8	9	10

Challenge 11

What's Your Attitude Toward Managing Change?

FANTASIES ABOUT CHANGE

Organizational transition is slow, expensive, and difficult. There is a tendency to believe that change can be instant, painless, and quick. Managers often seem to expect that changes they make will:

1) Not be disruptive.

2) Not cost much and be quick to implement.

3) Solve previous organizational problems.

These myths may help you understand why many organizations do such a poor job of managing the process of change, or become reluctant to accept the challenge of other changes, if previous attempts have gone badly.

The process of making a major change to an organization's culture requires people to let go of ''how it was'' and move through a period of doubt and uncertainty. When you are managing this process it becomes all-consuming and must be managed sensitively. Organizations that successfully handle the process of changing an organization's culture reduce the time required for similar changes in the future.

Change is often nothing more than a simple shift of technology, or some reporting relationships. But when major change hits a company, or a severe crisis demands a response, what really is changing is the ''corporate culture.'' The way the organization has been doing things. This much change demands a major shift in the way in which the work gets done. It is no longer possible to remain a caretaker, set in your ways. Rather, the challenge is often to increase productivity, while moving a work group in a new direction.

> LIKE A SOCCER COACH WHO FINDS HIS TEAM DOWN TWO GOALS AT THE END OF THE FIRST HALF, MANAGERS NEED A NEW GAME PLAN WHEN UNANTICIPATED CHANGES ARRIVE BEFORE THE FISCAL YEAR IS OVER.

THE ROLE OF THE MANAGER DURING CHANGE*

In times of change each manager, supervisor, and team leader will be called upon to lead change in his or her group. Top management should not be expected to manage the transition of individual work groups. Many middle managers wait for their leaders to tell them what to do. In many cases communication between top executives and middle managers is poor and there is no strategy to effectively announce and implement the change.

Managers want answers. When there are no ready solutions they often blame top management for leaving them in the dark. The best advice for these managers is to stop waiting and become a leader of their team. If they sit around waiting, the wave of change may wash over them and drown them. To stay afloat they must learn to manage change. Change offers both uncertainty *and* opportunity for them as managers. How they manage themselves and their work groups will make all of the difference.

Going through any major change will challenge the way we view ourselves. Major changes can be like the death and rebirth of a company. Living through this process is similar to a major remodeling of a kitchen. To obtain the final result you want, you first must rip out the old kitchen, leaving a lot of basic structure and emptiness. Then you begin to bring in new cabinets and appliances so they fit coherently. Once you add the final touches you can move back in and feel comfortable and productive again. It always takes longer than you thought it would and costs more than you estimated.

*Exerpts from the Fifty-Minute book *Managing Change at Work* by Cynthia D. Scott, Ph.D. and Dennis T. Jaffe, Ph.D. will be found on this and the following page.

BASIC GUIDELINES DURING CHANGE

The following are guidelines for changing corporate or team culture. You should:

1. Have a good reason for making the change

Culture changes are usually not fun. Take them seriously. Make sure you understand why you are making the change and that it is necessary.

2. Involve people in the change

People who are involved are less likely to resist. Being a part of the planning and transition process gives people a sense of control. Ask for opinions about how they would do it. Consider conducting surveys, focus groups, and polls.

3. Put a respected person in charge of the process

Each change needs a leader. Select someone who is seen in a positive light by the group.

4. Create transition management teams

You need a cross-section of your group, to plan, anticipate, troubleshoot, coordinate, and focus the change efforts.

5. Provide training in new values and behavior

People need guidance in understanding what the "new way" consists of and why it is more desirable. Training brings groups together. It allows them to express their concerns and reinforce newly learned skills.

6. Bring in outsider help

For some reason, there is often more power in what an outsider says than the same suggestions coming from inside. Use this power to reinforce the direction you want to go.

7. Establish symbols of change

Encourage the development of newsletters, new logos or slogans, and/or recognition events to help celebrate and reflect the change.

8. Acknowledge and reward people

As change begins to work, take time to recognize and recall the achievements of the people who made it happen. Acknowledge the struggle and sacrifices people have made.

CASE # 11: PROTECTIVE

Ryan is a most protective manager. He strives to keep his employees pressure free so that they will keep their personal productivity at a high level. Deep down, Ryan also wants to be liked and respected.

Yesterday, at a special management meeting, it was announced that everyone should be prepared for a major downsizing program that would help make the company "more lean" to compete for the projected future waves of change. After digesting everything he heard, Ryan has decided to take a middle-of-the road approach and follow this strategy:

- Absorb the big waves of change himself so he need pass on only the small waves to his "team" of nine employees.

- Have faith in the company's financial health to survive the "down period" and do business as usual in the department.

- Accept the premise that change is less destructive when it comes in "little doses" to those on the front line.

Do you agree with Ryan that it is to benefit all concerned for him to create an "umbrella of protection" over his employees? See if the author agrees with Ryan, page 104.

_____

_____

_____

_____

MANAGER'S SELF-INVENTORY SCALE

From Change to Challenge

In rating yourself on your ability to manage change, please take the following into consideration.

- People need time to adjust to change so the more communication that takes place among those involved the better. Talking about something that may or may not occur helps most people adjust if reality sets in.

- Not only does a department need a contingency option, individuals also need career "Plan B's" in case their job is eliminated. A good manager does not hide the possibility of change; he or she helps employees plan their personal career moves should a change be necessary.

- Implementing a major change is something like remodeling a home while living in it.

- Those who adjust to change should be given rewards for their efforts.

Please circle 6, 7, or 8 on the scale if you feel you could do an excellent job of managing a major reorganization of your department. Circle 3, 4, or 5 if you think you could do an average job. Circle 1 or 2 if you feel you could not handle it. If you have already managed a major change in an excellent manner, it is okay to circle 10.

SELF-DEVELOPMENT SCALE
Managing Change

Low									High
1	2	3	4	5	6	7	8	9	10

What Is Your Leadership Quotient?

ONLY SOLID MANAGERS ARE
FREE TO LEAD

Leadership at any level is built on basic management skills. Until an operation is well-managed, the person in charge is not sufficiently free to lead. Thus those attempting to lead without fundamental management competencies usually fail before they get started.

> "You can't lead an organization if you are constantly putting out management-related fires."
>
> "Some weeks it is all I can do to act as a caretaker around here. Lead? You've got to be kidding."
>
> "I feel apologetic about the fact that I can free myself to lead only now and then."

A few individuals are in a high enough position to select and train good administrative personnel who can free them to lead. But a first level manager who desires to lead must learn to manage efficiently in such a way that she or he has the freedom to add the leadership dimension to their style. This means that managers who want to lead need to free themselves by *being good at the first eleven categories in this book.*

What are the dangers of reaching into leadership behaviors before excellent management practices are in position?

• It is possible to wind up in limbo and lose your management job.

• Confusing leadership with management skills can leave you (the would-be leader) frustrated.

• Employees can feel insecure or lose respect for the way you operate.

First things first. Hone your management skills before jumping into leadership situations.

DIFFERENCES BETWEEN MANAGERS AND LEADER/MANAGERS

Explaining the differences between managers and leaders can be difficult to define. Recognizing this, the following statements may help you distinguish your dimensions of leadership. Place a ☑ in the appropriate box depending on whether you agree or disagree with the following statements:

AGREE	DISAGREE	
☐	☐	A good manager is content to simply follow directions and suggestions from above. A Leader/Manager is more apt to consider the future, and anticipate needs, problems and issues before being told that action is needed.
☐	☐	A good manager is willing to accept responsibility. A Leader/Manager seeks responsibility.
☐	☐	An effective manager will take modest risks (when the odds are favorable). A Leader/Manager accepts higher risks when they have the potential to result in greater progress, and commits to a plan of action with greater determination.
☐	☐	A Leader/Manager has more of an ''entrepreneurial spirit'' than a basic manager.
☐	☐	A manager is more apt to accept comfortable assignments while a leader looks for more demanding opportunities to demonstrate his or her leadership potential.
☐	☐	A manager usually views those under his or her supervision as employees. A leader views employees as team members and followers.
☐	☐	A basic difference between managers and leaders is attitude. Many managers are content to set modest goals, pacify others, try for a comfortable working environment and use power cautiously. A leader tends to set more demanding goals, challenges others, and creates a more dynamic working environment.

LEADERSHIP POTENTIAL SCALE

Even if you already occupy an important management position, you may wonder whether or not you have the potential to lead others. This exercise is designed to help you reach this decision. Read the statement at both ends of the scale and then circle the number that best indicates where you belong. Most people fall somewhere between the two extremes.

	HIGH	LOW
I can be both an excellent manager and have time to lead.	10 9 8 7 6 5 4 3 2 1	I am satisfied being a good manager.
I am a visionary. I love to plan for long-term goals.	10 9 8 7 6 5 4 3 2 1	Getting by one day at a time is my goal.
Risk-taking is my cup of tea. It challenges me.	10 9 8 7 6 5 4 3 2 1	I avoid risks whenever possible.
It is a challenge to discipline others.	10 9 8 7 6 5 4 3 2 1	I do not enjoy having to discipline others.
I enjoy communication and have the potential to become outstanding.	10 9 8 7 6 5 4 3 2 1	My communication skills are adequate.
I have the desire to become a top leader.	10 9 8 7 6 5 4 3 2 1	I'm comfortable as a follower.
I enjoy making tough decisions.	10 9 8 7 6 5 4 3 2 1	Decisions can be frustrating and scary.
I seek and welcome more responsibility	10 9 8 7 6 5 4 3 2 1	I avoid added responsibilities.
I can handle the pressure of being in the limelight under fire.	10 9 8 7 6 5 4 3 2 1	Pressure is not for me.
I believe I have the personality to become a successful leader.	10 9 8 7 6 5 4 3 2 1	Sorry, I'm not the leadership type.

TOTAL ☐

If you scored 80 or above, it would appear that you have a high desire and potential to be a leader. A rating between 60 and 80 shows good potential. A rating under 60 is a signal you may wish to delay weaving leadership practices into your management style.

CASE # 12: PROMOTION

Veronica is recognized by her superiors as an outstanding manager. Her reputation is so good, in fact, that she is being considered as a vice president. The only factor that has not fully satisfied a few involved in the decision is Veronica's leadership potential. Those who wish to keep her as a manager talk about:

- How important it is to keep her as an excellent "manager" role model for others.

- If she failed as a leader, it would be difficult to move back into pure management.

- Veronica has not taken a leadership course or seminar and might be underestimating what it takes.

- It might be best to give her another raise and keep her as an outstanding manager and hire a proven leader from the outside.

Those who wish to give her the promotion talk about:

- Promoting Veronica is a good risk and would encourage other women to follow.

- It would give recognition to the firm's Promotion From Within policy.

- It would keep Veronica in the firm instead of losing her to an outside organization.

- Veronica could train more excellent managers from her leadership role.

- Good managers are easier to come by than good leaders.

- Seeing the emergence of leadership qualities in her work.

Should Veronica be given the promotion? Why?

_____

_____

_____

Does the author agree with you? See page 104.

MANAGER'S SELF-INVENTORY SCALE

Many Managers—Few Leaders

Leadership is not an automatic extension of being a good manager. Those who do not see the difference (and refuse to study leadership as a separate process) often fail as leaders when, as managers, they were outstanding. As you prepare to rate yourself as a leader, place a check in the appropriate box preceeding each of the following statements:

TRUE   **FALSE**

☐ ☐ Leaders are willing to take more risks than managers.

☐ ☐ Leaders are forced to make tougher decisions.

☐ ☐ Leaders need to develop ''personality power'' so that they can convert employees into followers.

☐ ☐ A leader is always on stage—once you become a true leader people expect you to be ''up'' at all times.

☐ ☐ Leaders need vision and must articulate goals that followers will strive to reach.

SELF-DEVELOPMENT SCALE
Leadership

Low									High
1	2	3	4	5	6	7	8	9	10

MOST HIGHLY EFFECTIVE LEADER/MANAGERS ARE BORN DURING CHALLENGING TIMES.

PART

II

Constructing Your Profile

STEPS TO TAKE

Now that you have rated yourself on the twelve critical questions presented throughout this book, you can build your personal management skills profile. This will allow you to gain a better perspective regarding your managerial strengths and weaknesses.

Step 1: Study the profile sheet on the next page. Notice the twelve categories at the top, the scale from 1 to 10 on the left, and the squares at the bottom with page numbers assigned.

Step 2: Return to the pages numbered and record the scores (from 1 to 10) you previously assigned.

Step 3: On the scale at the left, locate the level on the column that equals the number at the bottom. Place a dot at this point.

Step 4: Connect the dots and you have completed your profile.

INVENTORY PROFILE SHEET

	PLANNING	DELEGATING	CONTROLLING	GOAL-SETTING	COACHING/COUNSELING	STAFFING
HIGH 10						
9						
8						
7						
6						
5						
4						
3						
2						
LOW 1						
Rating						
Page Numbers	8	14	20	27	35	42

TEAM-BUILDING	NEGOTIATING	PROBLEM SOLVING	PROFESSIONALISM	MANAGING CHANGE	LEADERSHIP	
						10 HIGH
						9
						8
						7
						6
						5
						4
						3
						2
						1 LOW
						Rating
49	56	63	71	79	87	Page Numbers

Rate Your Skills As A Manager

SAMPLE
INVENTORY PROFILE SHEET

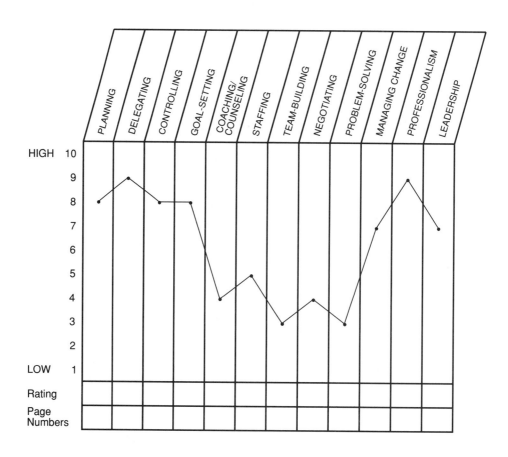

INTERPRETATION:

In rating 12 different management competencies, it is natural and expected that a few low scores emerge. It is a rare case when no improvement is indicated. In this profile, it would appear the individual is strong in job-oriented matters (planning, controlling, etc.) but somewhat weaker in people-oriented categories. Improvements in counseling/coaching, team-building, and problem-solving categories could go a long way in upgrading the performance of the individual manager and thus the productivity of departmental employees. Attending a seminar or reading a self-help book on team-building could pay handsome profits to the person behind this profile.

SAMPLE
INVENTORY PROFILE SHEET

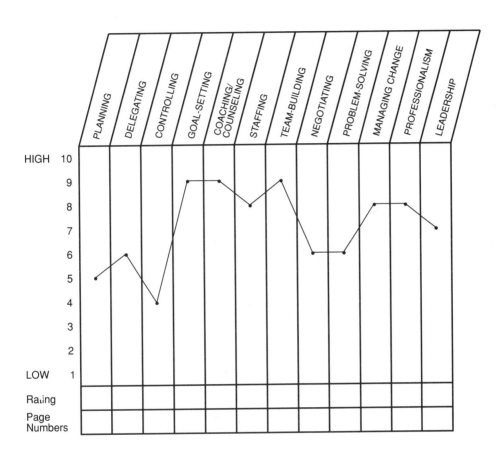

INTERPRETATION:

This profile indicates that the individual is outstanding in dealing with people but appears to be less effective in planning and controlling the operation itself. This may be a signal that a better balance between providing structure and developing human resources is needed.

The comparative low rating (6) in the delegating column is difficult to reconcile with the high ratings (9) in goal-setting, counseling, coaching, and team-building. People high in these categories are usually superior in delegating tasks to others.

The over-all high ratings (only column 3 under a 5) is impressive but improvement in the five modestly weak areas could make this individual even a stronger, more effective manager.

SAMPLE
INVENTORY PROFILE SHEET

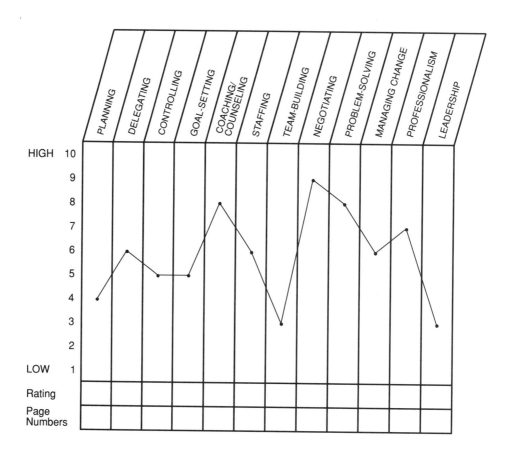

INTERPRETATION:

This profile sends a signal that the individual may be new and somewhat inexperienced in a management role and has yet to understand and prepare for the full spread of responsibilities normally found. At this juncture, the manager may be receiving plans from superiors and neglecting departmental planning. The same may be true of departmental goal-setting. It also appears that this individual may not have been exposed and trained in the benefits of team-building. The unusually low score in leadership may indicate that, at this stage, becoming a good, balanced manager is all the person can handle. Leadership can come later.

If the above interpretation is incorrect, then the person has many opportunities for improvement and could benefit from a series of management seminars.

P A R T

III

Interpreting
Your Profile

PROFILE INSIGHTS

What can you learn from the profile you just completed that will enhance your capacity to manage more effectively? Many insightful discoveries are possible if you follow these tips:

- Accept the fact that your profile is yours and yours *alone.* It reflects some of your strengths and weaknesses as a manager. It is not a scientific instrument, but it puts you into a more favorable position to see where improvements are needed.

- There is no such thing as a ''model'' profile. Field testing indicates that all managers have at least one weak area.

- It is highly beneficial to compare and discuss your profile with that of another manager with whom you have a good relationship. If this is not convenient, compare your profile with those on pages 94, 95, and 96. Interpretations by the author will be found on each profile sheet.

- It is normal for a manager to have eight or more rather high categories and two or three weak areas that have been ''blind spots'' keeping the individual from reaching his or her full potential. Often these weak spots have a subtle and negative impact upon categories where the individual would otherwise excel.

- The more one studies and compares her or his profile the more valuable insights can be gained.

More and more ambitious managers are turning to self-help books to enhance their careers. You are invited to investigate those listed on the next page.

HELP AHEAD

Rate Your Skills As A Manager

IMPROVING NEGLECTED AREAS

A single CRISP fifty minute book is referenced to each of the twelve profile categories below. Although the reader is encouraged to read on each subject from many sources, only the CRISP book that should be most helpful has been selected. You are invited to check your weak areas and consider the book recommended.

PROFILE CATEGORY	FIFTY MINUTE BOOK
CREATIVE PLANNING ☐	*Plan Your Work—Work Your Plan* Author: James Sherman, Ph.D.
DELEGATING ☐	*Delegating For Results* Author: Robert B. Maddux
CONTROLLING ☐	*Managing Disagreement Constructively* Author: Herbert S. Kindler, Ph.D.
GOAL SETTING ☐	*Effective Performance Appraisals* Author: Robert B. Maddux
COACHING/COUNSELING ☐	*Coaching and Counseling* Author: Marianne Minor
STAFFING ☐	*High Performance Hiring* Author: Robert Wendover, Ph.D.
TEAM BUILDING ☐	*Team Building* Author: Robert Maddux
NEGOTIATING ☐	*Successful Negotiation* Author: Robert Maddux
PROBLEM SOLVING ☐	*Team Problem Solving* Author: Sandy Pokras, Ph.D.
MANAGING CHANGE ☐	*Managing Change at Work* Authors: Cynthia D. Scott, Ph.D. and Dennis T. Jaffe, Ph.D.
PROFESSIONALISM ☐	*Quality At Work* Authors: Diane Bone & Rick Griggs
LEADERSHIP ☐	*Learning to Lead* Authors: Pat Heim, Ph.D. & Elwood Chapman

TAKING ACTION

The primary purpose of the management profile you have just completed is to help you identify one or more weak areas that are slowing down your progress. Now that you know where to concentrate your efforts, substantial and immediate improvements can be demonstrated.

Experience shows that for most people:

- Trying to improve in too many areas at the same time results in confusion and lack of motivation to continue.

- Concentrating on gaining knowledge in a single area (delegating, problem solving, etc.) for a period of one week produces the best results. Then look for chances to apply what you have learned, evaluating your performance as you proceed.

You may wish to complete the chart below and post it where it can act as a reminder. Start with the weakest of your weak areas and continue until you have brought all areas up to a more satisfactory level.

WEEKLY SELF-IMPROVEMENT SCHEDULE

Week #1: _____
                         (category)

Week #2: _____
                         (category)

Week #3: _____
                         (category)

Week #4: _____
                         (category)

SUGGESTED ANSWERS TO CASES

CASE #1: DECISION   Based upon the details presented, the limited planning by Victor is totally inadequate for the following reasons. (1) Victor may pass-over the appraisal forms too quickly. (2) He is not planning on getting ideas on how to make a smooth transition from the employees. (3) It might be better to simply mention that formal appraisals are coming up soon and everyone will be measured to some extent on their performance under the handicap of remodeling. (4) So far, Victor has not come up with a plan that will help waiters protect their ''tip'' income.

CASE #2: OVERSTATEMENT   The author defends Jeff because many managers have a ''blind spot'' about their ability to delegate. Effective delegating involves communication skills, work schedules, motivation, and many other aspects of good management. Delegating is, in many respects, the essence of good management. In the opinion of the author, the consultant was only trying to convince participants that they *should* give delegating more attention.

CASE #3: PREFERENCE   The author believes that there is a flaw in each of the styles. From the sparse data presented, it would appear that Herb allows his employees to drift too far into a permissive working environment (and possibly lower productivity) before he ''tightens up his discipline line.''

The flaw in Kathleen's style may be that her regular discipline line is too tight thus causing a loss in both creativity and productivity. However, if being ''on top of things'' means she exercises good control but does not stifle those who work for her, the flaw may not exist.

CASE #4: ATTITUDE   John is forgetting that he is not married to his firm. An economic recession provides disappointments but it also provides new challenges. John should set a new goal of finding a better managing opportunity—perhaps a different kind of firm that is expanding. Also, John needs to realize that his attitude belongs to him alone and if he does not keep it upbeat he is victimizing himself.

CASE #5: INTERVENTION   I would use coaching techniques with Jack in the hope I could slow him down so that he builds stronger relationships with co-workers as he builds his own career. My approach would be to use a hypotheical case of an individual similar to Jack who was unable to reach his goals because he had turned too many people against him.

I would attempt to get into a position where I could use counseling techniques with Jane. My approach would be as supportive as possible and should she volunteer to discuss a personal problem, I would be a good listener and hopefully assist her in finding her own solution.

CASE #6: CHOICE   The author would select 2, 3, and 6 as top priority possibilities. The remaining four, however, remain important considerations.

CASE #7: CRITERIA   The three primary criteria might be: (1) The sensitivity to lead without being heavy-handed about it. (2) Setting and communicating goals that involve the participation of all team members. (3) Giving each member a feeling of personal growth as part of the team. Based upon these criteria, Sandy appears to be the best prospect.

CASE #8: STYLE   Both Malcolm and Marci could be effective as negotiators. Malcom might be more effective in a firm that does business with ''hard'' and less ethical negotiators. Marci might do best with a firm that likes to keep negotiations at a highly professional level that would be more in harmony with their special clients and resources. Just because Marci hopes to avoid conflict situations does not mean she couldn't handle them should they surface.

CASE #9: EXPANSION   The author recommends following the six step procedure outlined on page 59. As part of the process, keep your superior informed and toward the end of your research and before you make your final decision, talk it over once more. Then submit your recommendations directly to the CEO as directed.

CASE #10: BEHAVIOR First, counsel with your friend on taking time off from work to get professional help from a recognized treatment center. Suggest that the individual acknowledge the problem to upper management. Second, if the individual does not act, offer to go with him or her to management to work out a solution. Third, if the person is unwilling to take any action, state you will have to withdraw your personal support.

CASE #11: PROTECTIVE By over-protecting his employees Ryan is not preparing them for the changes that are coming. Employees need to know what is going to happen. A few may wish to make a change. Others might wish to re-think their retirement dates. Only by ''open discussion'' can healthy adjustments be made.

CASE #12: PROMOTION Yes, Veronica should be given the promotion even though some risk is involved. She appears to be ready for additional growth as an executive. The firm could pay for on-campus leadership training or provide self-instructional materials. Also, having a mentor would be most important for a few months.

NOTES

NOTES

NOTES

NOTES

NOTES

NOTES

OVER 150 BOOKS AND 35 VIDEOS
AVAILABLE IN THE 50-MINUTE SERIES

We hope you enjoyed this book. If so, we have good news for you. This title is part of the best-selling *50-MINUTE*™ *Series* of books. All *Series* books are similar in size and identical in price. Many are supported with training videos.

To order *50-MINUTE* Books and Videos or request a free catalog, contact your local distributor or Crisp Publications, Inc., 1200 Hamilton Court, Menlo Park, CA 94025. Our toll-free number is (800) 442-7477.

50-Minute Series Books and Videos Subject Areas . . .

Management
Training
Human Resources
Customer Service and Sales Training
Communications
Small Business and Financial Planning
Creativity
Personal Development
Wellness
Adult Literacy and Learning
Career, Retirement and Life Planning

Other titles available from Crisp Publications in these categories

Crisp Computer Series
The Crisp Small Business & Entrepreneurship Series
Quick Read Series
Management
Personal Development
Retirement Planning